THE FREUD ANNIVERSARY
LECTURE SERIES
THE NEW YORK PSYCHOANALYTIC
INSTITUTE

THE FREUD ANNIVERSARY LECTURE SERIES

The New York Psychoanalytic Institute

PSYCHOTIC CONFLICT AND REALITY

Edith Jacobson, M.D.

INTERNATIONAL UNIVERSITIES PRESS, INC.

New York

This is an expanded version of the Lecture given at
The New York Academy of Medicine on May 11, 1965

Contents

Psychotic Conflict and Reality

THE SUBJECT which I have selected for this lecture involves problems in the area of psychotic disorders, a psychopathology whose study Freud hoped would throw more light onto the early developmental stages of the ego. Since Freud regarded patients suffering from psychoses to be inaccessible to psychoanalytic treatment, he explored the psychoses less comprehensively than the neuroses. However, his papers and comments on the psychoses (1911, 1914, 1924a, 1924b) are milestones in the development of a psychoanalytic theory of psychosis and have remained the basis on which all further analytic investigation of this broad group of mental disturbances has rested.

I shall deal with only one facet of these disorders: the psychotic's relation to the external world and the role that reality plays in the psychotic conflict.

Let me first clarify precisely what I mean by "psychotic" in contrast to "neurotic" conflict.

We remember that in the two brief papers on

"Neurosis and Psychosis" (1924a) and "The Loss of Reality in Neurosis and Psychosis" (1924b) Freud tried for the first time to employ the new structural concepts that he had developed in *The Ego and the Id* (1923) for a comparison of and distinction between neuroses and psychoses. In the first paper, Freud referred back to his previous discussions of "the disturbance in the relationship between the ego and the external world" in psychotics and neurotics. In his paper "On Narcissism" (1914) Freud had emphasized that, in the case of neurosis, we should speak not of a withdrawal from reality, but rather of an "introversion." In neurotics, he stated, the cathexes of the object representations, i.e., the impulses, feelings, fantasies related to "objects and things," are maintained, whereas the psychotic actually withdraws the cathexis from the objects and turns it to his own self. Consequently, Freud regarded the hypochondriacal anxiety of the psychotic as an expression of dammed-up narcissistic libido—in analogy to the anxiety in actual neurosis, an anxiety which develops from dammed-up object libido. He then distinguished three groups of phenomena in the psychotic: first, the residual phenomena, representing the normal or neurotic part of his personality; secondly, the phenomena representing the morbid processes, i.e., the processes of regression, the withdrawal from the objects, the megalomania, the hypochondriacal anxiety, and the affective dis-

[8]

turbances in general; and thirdly, the processes of restitution by means of which the psychotic tries to reattach his libido to objects in a manner corresponding to yet different from that used in neurosis. These restitutive processes are responsible for the stormy overt psychotic manifestations.

We realize that this paper on narcissism was written before Freud developed his second anxiety theory, his structural hypotheses, and his new conceptions of the role of the aggressive drives. Thus, in the two 1924 papers, Freud did not return to the previous formulations. In "Neurosis and Psychosis," Freud stated that in both neurosis and psychosis the factors precipitating the illness are the same—a frustration. However, "The pathogenic effect depends on whether, in a conflictual tension of this kind, the ego remains true to its dependence on the external world and attempts to silence the id, or whether it lets itself be overcome by the id and thus torn away from reality" (p. 151). At the end of this paper, Freud furthermore raised "the question of what the mechanism, analogous to repression, can be by means of which the ego detaches itself from the external world. This [he stated] cannot, I think, be answered without fresh investigations; but such a mechanism, it would seem, must, like repression, comprise a withdrawal of the cathexis sent out by the ego" (p. 153).

In "The Loss of Reality in Neurosis and Psychosis" (1924b), Freud answered this question. He made clear that he referred to the mechanism of denial or disavowal: "neurosis does not disavow the reality, it only ignores it; psychosis disavows it and tries to replace it" (p. 185).

This conception of Freud's—that, in neurosis, the conflict is between the ego and the id; in psychosis, between the ego and reality—has certainly been amply confirmed. However, it is noteworthy that Freud, who at that time was concerned mainly with structural formulations, spoke only in general terms of the ego, the id, and reality. He did not consider the specific nature of the instinctual and narcissistic conflicts preceding and inducing the psychotic's break with reality. In the ensuing discussion these intrapsychic conflicts will be referred to as "psychotic conflicts."

Hartmann (1953) supplemented and elaborated Freud's statements on psychoses from the ego-psychological and economic points of view. First of all, Hartmann stressed not only "the rival claims made by the id and the external world upon the ego (Freud 1940, p. 114)," but, in particular, the impairment of the ego itself, of its defenses and functions, including the formation of affects. In this connection, he mentioned Katan's (1954) quest for a closer study of the "residual personality" and of those ego functions that remain intact in schizophrenics—a point that is of particular relevance to the subject of this lecture.

In his discussion of the instinctual aspects and

their interaction with the ego aspects in psychosis, Hartmann called attention to the deneutralization of the drives and, in particular, to the damaging effect that the deneutralization of aggression has on the superego and on the defenses and counter-cathectic formations. This deneutralization, on the one hand, weakens the defenses of the ego and, on the other, liberates and thus increases the free aggression generally found in psychotics.

This is certainly a convincing assumption, except that the deneutralization of the sexual and aggressive drives cannot sufficiently account for the intensity of the destructive forces that we observe in psychotics. In addition, Hartmann mentions the processes of drive defusion which may be combined with those of deneutralization. This is very important because, in contrast to the concept of deneutralization, Freud's idea of fusion and defusion of drives has bearing on the ambivalence conflicts which play such a prominent part in the psychotic's relations to the external world. But Hartmann intentionally avoided discussing the special nature of the instinctual conflicts in psychosis, except for mentioning the narcissistic problems of the schizophrenic and his vulnerability to narcissistic injuries.

Pertinent in this connection is Freud's statements, in "Mourning and Melancholia" (1917), about the melancholic's narcissistic fixations which predispose him to his narcissistic withdrawal and

[11]

his narcissistic identification with the disappointing love object. However, in their discussions of the manic-depressive states, Freud and Abraham (1924) also emphasized the libidinal impoverishment of the melancholic and his severe ambivalence conflicts, which cause the retreat from the external world and the "inner object loss." These considerations certainly also apply—and may be even more valid—in the case of schizophrenia, and are especially significant from the dynamic point of view.

In fact, persons who tend to develop psychotic states regularly show a characteristic combination of primitive narcissistic and (pregenital) sadomasochistic fixations which predispose them to dangerous hostility conflicts of a kind that are not found in neurotics (see Bak, 1954).

Hence, one of the most impressive features of the intrapsychic psychotic conflict is the struggle between active and passive, sadistic and masochistic, destructive and self-destructive tendencies, and in general between sexual and aggressive impulses, which at certain stages of the illness may be used as defenses against each other (Jacobson, 1957).

On the basis of clinical observations of manic-depressive, schizophrenic, and certain toxic psychoses, I feel even tempted to raise the question whether the rise of aggression at the expense of libido may not be the primary agent that induces the general deneutralization of the drives and the regressive processes in all areas of the psychic organization. It is a fact that neurotic patients can display an amazing sexualization of certain ego functions—especially creative functions—without marked impairment of these functions and of the ego in general. In contrast, we hardly ever see enduringly undisturbed functioning in patients whose ego and superego functions are in the service of destructive goals. In any case, the severity of the hostility conflicts accounts for the psychotic's predominant fears. Whereas the central fear of the neurotic is castration fear, the psychotic is afraid of an impending dissolution of the psychic structure—involving a partial or total breakdown of object and self representations and resulting in a withdrawal from the external world to the point of manifest psychotic symptom formation.

Whatever the final answer to these problems may be, the inferences that could be drawn from Freud's statements regarding the defectiveness of the ego's repressive barriers in the psychotic, the disintegration and dedifferentiation of the psychic structures, the fixation at early narcissistic (and pregenital) stages, the regressive return to such primitive positions, and the propensity for using denial and other primitive defense mechanisms—all these have been confirmed by clinical observations and further psychoanalytic explorations.

However, this does not imply that a satisfactory agreement has been reached on the extent and na-

[13]

ture of the disturbance in the psychotic's relation
to the external world. We remember the rather
controversial views on the psychotic's capacity for
personal object relationships. Whereas Freud
(1916-1917) emphasized the inability of schizophrenics to develop a transference relationship,
others thought differently and concentrated on psychotherapeutic or even psychoanalytic work with
psychotics, including severe hospitalized cases.[1]
Comparing the methods used by the various analysts in their therapeutic approach to psychotics,
we find, moreover, that their treatment techniques
differ a great deal and that their opinions on this
issue are often quite contradictory.[2] In spite of
this, there now exists rather general agreement on
the fact that many types of schizophrenics are able,
at least at certain stages of their illness, to establish an enduring relationship to their therapists.
Some patients, whose egos are comparatively intact, may even develop a true analytic process,
while others may need a modified and specific kind
of psychotherapeutic technique. I shall return to
the treatment problems at the end of this lecture.

Yet even such clinical experiences do not tend to
confirm the rather extreme view, held, e.g., by

[1] See, e.g., Federn (1952), Freeman et al. (1958, 1965), Knight
(1939, 1953), Eissler (1953), Sullivan (1953), Fromm-Reichmann
(1939, 1948), Lidz and Lidz (1952), Wexler (1953), Little (1958),
Rosenfeld (1965), Searles (1960, 1965a).

[2] See, e.g., the papers contained in *Psychotherapy with Schizophrenics* (Brody and Redlich, 1952).

[14]

Waelder (1960), who spoke of the warm, affectionate object relations that can, supposedly, be seen in many psychotics. In view of the deterioration of superego and ego, it is altogether questionable whether in certain types of schizophrenia, or at certain stages of the illness, we can speak in ordinary terms about the patient's emotional attitudes, as though his libidinal and destructive drive impulses would always find the same affective expression as in normal persons' feelings and feeling qualities. Even when psychotics show emotional reactions, these are frequently difficult to understand, and such terms as "love" and "hate" may have a very different meaning to them than they do to us. For this reason the therapist's empathy with psychotic patients is put to such severe tests.

With regard to the general ego functions and the psychotic's relations to the inanimate object world, the picture is equally puzzling. There are delusional psychotics who, despite their impaired reality testing in the areas of their psychopathology, may be able, for instance, temporarily to engage in highly intellectual work.[3] Other patients may show such a severe deterioration of their ego functions that they are incapable of working, even though they may not suffer from any overt psychotic symptoms such as delusions or hallucinations.

---

3 Eissler in his book on Goethe (1963), refers to such a patient who even during delusional psychotic episodes was able for a long time to do scientific research work.

In view of these contradictory observations and positions, we may well question the validity of any generalized statement about the psychotic's (especially the schizophrenic's) relations to the external world—to personal objects as well as to reality in general.[4] At this point we do well to remember Fenichel's cautious remarks in the chapter on schizophrenia: "The diversity of schizophrenic phenomena makes a comprehensive orientation more difficult than in any other class of mental disorders. . . . Certainly 'schizophrenia' is not a definite nosological entity, but rather embraces a whole group of diseases" (1945, p. 415). However, I believe that the difficulties to which I referred highlight even more the need for specialized studies, not only of all the different types of psychoses, but also of the various stages in the development of different disorders (Searles, 1965a).

I have found it very revealing, indeed, to explore the different relations to the external world, not only in florid psychotic cases, but especially in ambulatory mild schizophrenics, in patients showing a psychotic potential, and in patients who had suffered psychotic episodes in the past but were currently in a period of remission. I believe that studies of such patients' acting-out behavior, of their personal object relations, their sublimations, their attitudes to work and to their inanimate en-

4 See Hartmann (1956), Frosch (1966).

vironment can aid us in resolving at least some of the above-mentioned contradictions. They reveal, first of all, that it is a great oversimplification of the psychotic's complex relations to the external world if his conflict with reality is approached merely in terms of a break with reality and the ensuing restitutional phenomena. At certain stages of the illness, schizophrenics frequently develop very intense personal relations, which may—falsely—suggest a true capacity for love, warmth, and affection. Although these relations use or even rest on the intact or neurotic part of the personality, they may actually be an expression of the patient's special psychotic pathology and of the particular role that external objects and reality play in his psychotic conflicts. This is what I now wish to demonstrate.

In view of the limited number of psychotics that I could study, I must emphasize that I cannot possibly say how far my findings have general validity. My observations of such patients frequently reminded me of what Freud said in his paper on "The Loss of Reality in Neurosis and Psychosis" (1924b): "We call behaviour 'normal' or 'healthy', if it combines certain features of both reactions [i.e., the neurotic and the psychotic]—if it disavows the reality as little as does a neurosis, but if it then exerts itself, as does a psychosis, to effect an alteration of that reality. Of course, this expedient, normal, behaviour leads to work being carried out on the external world; it does not stop, as in psychosis, at effecting inner changes. It is no longer *autoplastic* but *alloplastic*" (p. 185). I found these remarks, in which Freud compared the psychotic's efforts to effect on alteration of reality with the normal person's alloplastic endeavors, very inspiring. They made me wonder to what extent the psychotic, as long and inasmuch as he does relate to the external world, may attempt in his way to alter external reality in terms of adapting it, as it were, to his very special needs and purposes.

The normal person, too, tries to alter and to use reality for his need gratifications. However, his alloplastic efforts to alter reality are dominated by the reality principle, and his adjustment to reality is based on autoplastic as well as alloplastic devices. This is not the case in psychotics. Because of their unusual narcissistic vulnerability they are apt to experience any frustration as a narcissistic injury and to react to it with boundless narcissistic and hostility conflicts, which may accompany or may induce drive defusion and deneutralization and a general regression to primitive narcissistic positions. The resulting impairment of the psychic structures and defense organization leads to a further increase of free aggression, rendering the ego even less able to withstand the assault of the instinctual forces and especially that of the destructive and self-destructive (pregenital) drive impulses.

It seems to me that, in this situation, certain

types of psychotic patients will not immedia-
ately break with reality but will first attempt the
opposite: they try to turn to and to employ the
external world as an aid in their efforts to replen-
ish their libidinal resources, to strengthen their
weakening ego and superego, and to resolve their
narcissistic and instinctual conflicts with which
their defective ego cannot cope. This leads to a
more or less conspicuous acting-out behavior,
which may find many different forms of expression.
To be sure, neurotic patients, too, may try to externalize their conflicts and to resolve them with
help from without. However, a comparison shows
striking differences, which I shall briefly discuss
later on. At this point I only want to stress that, in
contrast to neurotic patients, psychotics tend to
use the external world for the purpose of preventing a dissolution of their ego and superego structures and a regressive dedifferentiation and
disintegration that would threaten them with a
manifest psychotic breakdown. For this reason they
may not only hold on, or even cling, to the external
world, but try to change it, to create one that will
suit their special needs, and to reject and deny
those aspects that are of no use to them. This view
does not contradict Freud's statement that in psychotics the conflict is one between the ego and
reality. However, I want to show that in this conflict the ego first makes tremendous efforts to re-

sort to or even to force reality to assist it in its hopeless struggle with the instinctual threats.

Psychotics give up reality and replace it by a newly created fantasy reality only if reality fails to lend itself to their purposes and to help them in their conflict solution.

Schizophrenic patients may spell this out rather clearly. Complaining about the incest taboo, one of them said very angrily: "I cannot accept this law. Not I, the world must change. That would resolve my conflict. And if it won't—to hell with the world!" Some psychotic patients assured me that they should be permitted to act out, because they needed it, and giving it up would "drive me crazy." A bisexual male schizophrenic maintained that homosexual activities were necessary and should be legalized, since without them he and persons like him would develop paranoid delusions —and in his case as well as that of other schizophrenics this was quite true.

I could quote a great number of psychotic patients whose remarks demonstrated not only their inability, but their unwillingness to accept and to adjust to reality, and their insistence on changing and adapting it to their purposes and on using it as a means to resolve their conflicts and to prevent a manifest psychosis.

However, the conflict situation in psychotics is certainly more complicated than these few drastic examples indicate. Let me present some clinical case material that might give a clearer picture of what I want to convey. I do not intend to discuss at length the special nature and origin of the patient's conflicts and pathology. The main goal of my report is to consider the patient's relations to the external world from the perspective of my thesis.

Case Illustration

The patient, Mr. A., was a criminal lawyer in his thirties, a junior partner in a very respectable law firm. He was the oldest of seven children, all born on the West Coast. His mother was a severely disturbed, probably schizophrenic person, who gradually deteriorated. His father showed conspicuous psychopathic trends. He was sexually promiscuous and a severe gambler. He finally separated from the family, which was left impoverished.

The father had played a protective role during the patient's childhood, when Mr. A. was exposed to his mother's sadistic and seductive attempts to turn him into a girl. She beat his penis when he had erections and repeatedly threatened him with circumcision. At the age of two and a half, Mr. A. had an almost fatal accident which was caused by the pregnant mother's lack of caution. The father had saved him by rushing him to a hospital, where he remained several weeks. On his return the boy discovered that a new child, a little sister, had arrived.

During Mr. A.'s prepuberty years, the mother began to talk to him about his father's sexual misconduct and told him that if he remained a "good," i.e., sexless, boy, she would later on live with him. When he began to have dates, she drastically interfered with them and kept him altogether away from girls. At that time the patient began to develop feminine mannerisms, which he himself disliked and successfully tried to overcome.

When he reached puberty, his mother became pregnant again and almost died in childbirth. At that time Mr. A. had conscious daydreams that if his mother died, he would replace her and take care of the family. Some time later, his father moved out of the parental bedroom and began to sleep in the same bed with Mr. A., with his legs around the boy's body. During this period he also made the patient work from morning to night, and gave him cruel beatings when he was disobedient. Under these circumstances, Mr. A. became an extremely submissive, hard-working boy, with conspicuous compulsive and masochistic features.

After a very traumatic primal scene experience in his adolescence, the boy's compulsive defenses broke down and his sadomasochistic identifications with the sick impulse-ridden parents erupted. When his father frankly expressed his suspicion that Mr. A. was having homosexual relations with a rather psychopathic younger boy, the patient actually started a homosexual affair with this friend, who had "a very big penis," and went with him on thrilling stealing adventures. The patient's delinquent behavior stopped abruptly, when he began openly to rebel against his parents and to blame them for their weaknesses. At this time he again became very compulsive, but also developed paranoid traits and the tendency to fight "for good causes." He finally detached himself from his family, left home, and returned only at times of severe financial and emotional crises to help the family, especially the younger siblings, who still look up to him as to their parent.

Unaided, Mr. A. worked his way through college and law school, and made a successful career in politics. His skill in manipulating people and in using them for his purposes was, indeed, quite outstanding. However, he frequently managed to provoke conflict situations, which revealed his paranoid trends. During such periods the patient would drink quite heavily and feel tempted to go on homosexual cruises, which I shall describe later. In general, he tried hard to live up to his ideal, which was to lead an asexual life. Occasionally, however, he had homosexual affairs, in which he always played the role of the sexual aggressor. At other times he was satisfied by observing the homosexual behavior of others. Since he had also slept a few times with women, he regarded himself as potentially bisexual. Although his homosexual problems were very disturbing to him, Mr. A. was able to sustain a rather precarious emotional balance.

However, encouraged by some friends, who complained about his rigid compulsive attitudes, the patient went to a psychiatrist for treatment. While he was in therapy, both of his parents died, shortly after he had had violent fights with them because of their irresponsible parasitical behavior. Although Mr. A. knew that his parents had both been physically very ill, he was convinced that his verbal attacks had killed them and felt very guilty. At that time, he began to lose control of himself and started to act out in a way that was somewhat reminiscent of his adolescent behavior. On his free evenings, he would feel so anxious and upset that he would rush away from home, drink, and go on homosexual binges with growing fears of an exposure, which his behavior actually invited. He soon found himself in a severe paranoid conflict situation with his superior, whose attitudes reminded him of those of his parents. The patient experienced states of panic, excitement, and confusion, and developed delusional ideas of persecution. He was convinced that his superior and his collaborators were plotting against him and intended to ruin and even to kill him. He barricaded himself in his room and kept a knife ready at his side to be prepared for the attacks of his persecutors. He had to be hospitalized for several months.

After his breakdown he gave up his political career, moved to the East Coast, and became a criminal lawyer.

When Mr. A. began his treatment with me, he seemed to enjoy an excellent professional reputation. He was known to be a brilliant but rather detached, distant, and compulsive person, a devoted and tireless worker, and a very clever and vigorous defender of his clients.

The patient himself was quite aware of, and often talked about, the very significant role that his professional work played in his psychic economy. In this connection he emphasized how glad he was that after his breakdown he had again been able to refrain, almost completely, from sexual activities, except for masturbation, which he disregarded since it did not involve a partner. What had helped him to live up to his conscious ideal and lead this so-called asexual ascetic life was his work and his friendship with a young man, who some years previously had moved into his apartment. His increasing conflicts with this young man, Charlie, had caused Mr. A. to seek treatment with me. Although many years ago he had seduced Charlie, the patient now had very intense but lofty feelings for him. In general, sex had to be excluded from his personal relations, and feelings from his sexual relations. But even his emotional attachments were devoid of affectionate feelings. He did not permit himself affection, which he regarded as feminine, whereas he considered aggressiveness a male characteristic.

Like his father and two former friends, the young man who lived with Mr. A. was a gifted, charming, but irresponsible, destructive, and self-destructive psychopath, who, moreover, physically resembled the patient's mother. Charlie was a dipsomaniac whose drinking bouts and homosexual escapades had on several occasions gotten him into serious troubles. It must also be noted that the patient's clients were mostly young male delinquents, whose asocial behavior had much in common with that of his friend. In his relationship to these young men, the patient assumed a part that he had already in his childhood begun to play with his younger siblings. It was the part of the parental guide, protector, and rescuer that he himself had so badly needed. Just as his clients and his younger siblings did, his young friend looked up to the patient as to a paternal figure, on whom he depended for practical, emotional, and sometimes financial support. Mr. A.'s efforts on behalf of Charlie were also quite similar to his work with his clients, whom he not only defended vigorously, but also tried to rehabilitate and to "rescue"—sometimes with amazing success.

In the case of Charlie, Mr. A.'s plan was to turn him into an "active" and heterosexual person, to cure him of his alcoholism, and thus to promote his social and vocational adjustment. This endeavor practically amounted to an additional job, which involved much time and great self-sacrifice. Mr. A.'s failure to achieve what he had planned gradually led to insoluble conflicts. He began to react to Charlie's relapses with increasing rage and ultimately separated from him. In these rages Mr. A. frequently developed paranoid ideas of jealousy. At such times he suspected Charlie of having affairs with "bitches," i.e., with older, passive, feminine men, who represented his own unacceptable passive homosexual wishes.

Although in the course of his treatment Mr. A. has become emotionally rather detached from this incurable young man, he still feels bound to him, treats him as a friend, and, as in the case of his family, comes to his help in times of emergency. He supported Charlie in making a successful vocational change, and was very amazed to discover that Charlie improved only after their separation.

What I have described so far does not sound in any way different from what we might observe in a neurotic patient. In fact, it was only after the patient had separated from his young friend that the deeper meaning and role of this friendship in the patient's emotional life, and the very regressive, narcissistic, and sadomasochistic level on which it had rested became fully apparent.

Mr. A. reacted to the separation from Charlie in a most striking way. He began to overload his days, his evenings, and his weekends with work. When he was nevertheless left with free time on his week-

[27]

ends, he became so restless, anxious, and agitated
that he would hurriedly leave home, drink, and go
on brief homosexual escapades with young male
prostitutes. Significantly, he never brought these
boys home and never took a drink while he worked.
In fact, he kept his sexual life and his drinking so
secret and so strictly isolated from his professional
life that nobody ever suspected that he was a homosexual. Since his homosexual adventures were
reminiscent of his acting out prior to his paranoid
episode, they left the patient not only with intense
guilt feelings, but also with increasing fears that he
might have another psychotic breakdown. He began to reproach himself for having "used" and
"harmed" his friend, instead of really helping him.
What he meant became clear when we understood
how much he had actually needed and used Charlie
—and his work as well—for the purpose of coping
with his own sexual, narcissistic, and especially his
profound hostility conflicts in order to maintain
his precarious emotional balance.

Precisely what had been the nature of this relationship?

Mr. A.'s paranoid conflicts and fears were rooted
in his sadomasochistic narcissistic relations, his
identifications and reactive counteridentifications
with his seductive and destructive parents.[5] These

[5] In the Simmel-Fenichel Lecture which I presented to the Los
Angeles Psychoanalytic Society and Institute, I discussed the
special nature of the patient's paranoid conflicts from a different
perspective (1966b).

had determined both his object choice and his vocational choice, as well as the various roles which he and his friend, or his clients, played in these relationships.

Even on the surface, it was clear that in Mr. A.'s mind Charlie was equated with his bad parents as well as with the homosexual, delinquent boy that he himself had been in the past and might at any time become again. Thus, his friend represented the illness—the "evil" that might befall him if his superego and his rigid, compulsive reaction formations were to break down and his fragile ego be overrun by the id.

The Use of Objects and Reality for Defensive Purposes

Let us now study how Mr. A. managed to use his intense and complex relations to his friend and his clients for the solution of his own conflicts.

In the course of his treatment the patient had characterized his parents' attitudes to him very pointedly: "My mother expected me to be 'a man without a penis,' whereas my father wanted me to be nothing but 'a boy with a penis,'" which meant not a person but simply "a penis," precisely what in his mind his father had been. These remarks implied that the patient's mother wanted him to lead a sexually completely abstinent, self-sacrificing life, while the promiscuous and sadistic father expected him to be completely unrestricted with regard to sex and aggression.

These irreconcilable and destructive parental attitudes and demands precluded any normal solution of his profound emotional and instinctual conflicts. Moreover, they threatened the patient not only with castration but, even worse, with a total loss of identity.

How did the patient meet these threats?

I have described that the patient's conscious moral standards reflected those handed down by his mother and that he tried to live up to them with the support of rigid and overly strict compulsive reactive formations. But in view of the paternal influences, these autoplastic defenses were bound to be very brittle and could be effective only temporarily. They were apt to break down whenever he was exposed to narcissistic hurts, and especially when people exploited his masochistic attitudes. Thus the patient had tried to resort, in addition, to a defensive operation that required the aid of external objects, the use of denial, and primitive introjective and projective mechanisms.

These mechanisms had the aim of reconciling the opposing parental demands and prohibitions, of renouncing as well as gratifying his instinctual wishes—to possess and use a penis and be a powerful manly person. These devices were generally rather effective and helped him maintain his emotional balance and an adjustment to a reality that he himself had partly "created." However, these same devices also predisposed him to acting out which, under special circumstances could deteriorate and even pave the way to a florid psychotic state.

Instead of himself being a boy with a penis, Mr. A. would defensively choose as a friend a boy with a penis, i.e., a penis that he could make a part of himself. Establishing a close relationship with such a boy, he could then assume the role of the powerful asexual man who owned and aggressively controlled this penis.

Here we may ask again in which way Mr. A.'s relationship to his friend differs from that of the narcissistic type of neurotic woman to her sexual partner, whom she has unconsciously turned into her penis. The difference has to do with the nature of the interpersonal relationship between the friends. It became clear when the patient explained the reasons why he could not tolerate affection and had to evade sexual relations with his friend—and with other young men whom he "liked." His equation of affection and femininity made any physical contact with them very threatening. He felt that emotional and physical "closeness" might tempt him to accept a passive-feminine masochistic position. Moreover, in view of the weak boundaries between himself and the other, he was even consciously afraid that this contact with a partner he liked might induce experiences of merging with

[31]

his partner, which might lead to feelings of loss of his own self and of loss of "control of the penis he owned." This, he feared, would result in a psychotic state.

The fact that in Mr. A.'s mind his friend was not an individual but merely a part of himself explains why the patient could refrain from sexual activities as long as this friendship lasted. Only after the separation did the patient become aware of the fact that he had secretly encouraged his friend's drinking bouts and the resulting homosexual escapades by offering him drinks and taking him to bars frequented by homosexuals. The intrapsychic act of turning himself and the friend into a symbiotic unit permitted the patient, at least in fantasy, to participate in the other's forbidden perverse activities. The model of this device was his reaction to the primal scene experiences to which he had repeatedly been exposed in early childhood. This participation granted the patient a vicarious pleasure that was great enough for him to renounce indulging in sexual activities himself. It turned out that even after the separation from his friend, when he himself went on homosexual escapades, his main pleasure was actually that of remaining in the role of an observer.

But he did not always remain only in the role of observer. He actively induced others to engage in certain activities, and this pattern as well had a forerunner in childhood. When he was a little boy he indulged in an acting out with his sister which was reminiscent of what he later did with Charlie. Seducing his sister to do forbidden things had helped him abstain from them himself. Instead, he enjoyed first her bad behavior, and then the resulting punishment by the mother, whom he regularly informed of his sister's evil deeds. By letting Charlie act out, Mr. A. could gratify his own sadomasochistic sexual impulses, and in particular his frightening passive homosexual desires. In this way the patient could, in addition, deny his own guilt, project it onto the other, blame Charlie for his bad behavior, and let Charlie take the punishment.

This explains the patient's reactions to the loss of his friend. I described how he tried to submerge himself in work, i.e., to replace the friendship by investing all his energy in his work with his clients. This certainly helped him sustain sufficient emotional control during his working hours, but when he had free time, his friend's absence had the prompt effect of throwing him back on homosexual acting out of his own. It was the same acting out which he had so frantically tried to cure in his friend. I need not emphasize that his affairs were devoid of any affectionate feelings. He always had to be the aggressor who got himself a boy, i.e., a big penis to be used and thrown away.

Thus it was quite true that Mr. A. had needed and used Charlie for his own defensive purposes.

At least part of the patient had not really wanted to rescue the friend, but had helped harm and ruin him. However, this was not the whole story. I have previously emphasized the degree to which this device aided the patient in leading what he felt to be a spotless, i.e., asexual and "good," life. This device, combined with the denial of his secret acting out and its motivations, enabled him to lend himself to his friend and to his clients as a model and as a kindly, helpful, but also morally demanding, restrictive, critical superego figure.

While their admiring, grateful, affectionate responses and his professional successes served Mr. A. as continuous sources of libidinal stimulation and raised his self-esteem, this parental role also offered him a further safety valve for his hostility. As a lawyer for the defense, he not only could fight for his clients against the authorities; his friend's and his clients' recurring relapses also allowed the patient to turn his criticism and his anger away from himself and to discharge them via these young men.

What I have described provides a key to an understanding of the sadomasochistic homosexual power struggle underlying all of the patient's significant relations. These served his purposes as long as he could sustain the part of the powerful figure, or even the omnipotent though benign agent, who owned and dominated but also served and sacrificed himself to these objects or their lives.

Actually, his struggle for this position of power and the acting out that it involved represented defensive operations. Their prerequisite was the regressive narcissistic nature of the patient's relations to these significant objects; the weakness of the boundaries between the psychic representations of these objects and his own self; the choice of a special type of work and suitable objects that lent themselves to an externalization of his conflicts; the primitive "global" projective identifications. All these enabled the patient to turn external objects into intolerable or desirable but unacceptable parts of his own self, which he could thus control and master. This presupposed concretization and personification of his own impulses, feelings, and character traits to a degree not found in neurotic behavior. While external objects could thus become representative of his defective superego, of his weak and guilt-ridden ego, of his penis, i.e., of his frightening id impulses, he would assume toward them the part of the powerful superego and the strong ego that they and he himself needed. Controlling these objects could then be equated with controlling himself. Changing them according to his wishes replaced or became identical with changing himself. Whenever he could achieve beneficial alterations in his clients, Mr. A. felt that these changes brushed off on himself. And they actually did, because he could then, as he put it, "reversely borrow" the strength and the conscience from the persons to whom he had lent them.

However, I must also emphasize the fact that Mr. A.'s personal relations were by no means limited to these primitive defensive identifications on which I have focused. His transference manifestations, his relations to his collaborators, and his attitude to his work revealed that with people whom he respected the patient was quite able to maintain relations on a more advanced level, and to establish selective identifications which had a constructive influence on his psychic structures. For this reason, his work, which offered him a certain amount of professional and personal contacts, actually fortified his superego, his ego, and its compulsive defenses. It strengthened his reality testing and enriched his emotional life.

Of particular significance was the fact that the patient's job revolved not only about personal relations with his clients. He also did a great deal of legal, administrative, and managerial work. This required abstract thought processes which were evidently highly cathected. He spent an inordinate amount of time and effort on "reorganizing" his work, a perpetual necessity in his eyes. Outside the area of his conflicts Mr. A. was surprisingly perceptive and frequently showed excellent judgment.

I wanted to emphasize the normal—or neurotic —traits of this patient, which were part of his "residual" personality, in order to show how closely interwoven they were with attitudes and actions which originated in his psychotic conflicts and served his defense against a psychotic breakdown. Some of Mr. A.'s special attitudes to his work further demonstrate the close interaction of "neurotic" and "psychotic" features. Essentially, the patient's relations to his clients were of the same narcissistic nature as those to his friend, except that he could keep himself more detached from his clients than from his friend. Because of his careful choice of "suitable" objects, he hardly distorted their real personality, although he ignored and scotomized those traits which were of no use to him. The number and variety of his cases helped the patient to reduce his emotional investment in any single client and to split off and divert his aggression to the hopeless cases. Only occasionally did he develop paranoid rages, either when his defense of a client was not effective, or when his clients, and especially their families, were uncooperative and could not be "mastered." The "mastery" of his work seemed to be such a particular challenge because work, i.e., his functioning, seemed to represent a concrete object which, being part of himself, he could keep under control, master, and change. Whereas previously Mr. A. had worked for special political "causes," he was now just as deeply concerned with specific legal "causes." The significant point is that he had to change and to master the world.

What I wanted to convey with the help of this case report is: the patient's relationship and frantic adherence to his work, his friend, and his clients; his compulsive tendency to fill his days and nights with overwork; his homosexual acting out when he was not occupied and was left to his own devices —all these become meaningful if we understand them in terms of his efforts to resolve his sexual narcissistic and hostility conflicts with the aid of the external world.

The question arises whether this patient is a unique case, and whether one can generalize from it. I am inclined to believe that a large group of psychotics highly invest and frantically adhere to a carefully chosen type of work, personal objects, and activities. These activities are employed in very much the same way and for the same purposes as they were in the patient described. Actually, such activities protect them for long periods from manifest psychotic episodes. Mr. A. belongs to a group of prepsychotic or ambulatory schizophrenic patients who first called my attention to the role that external objects play in their attempts to solve conflicts. This group consisted of male and female patients who held different jobs and pursued different professions. On the other hand, they had certain conspicuous features in common. Most of them were unmarried or divorced, or estranged from their families. Some sustained intense but very fragile erotic relations to which they desperately clung. Others were frantically concerned with their work and, like Mr. A., led a rather ascetic asexual life, which occasionally alternated with periods of intense heterosexual, homosexual, or bisexual acting out. On the whole, most of these patients tended to overburden themselves with work. Many functioned amazingly well and maintained their jobs or positions for long periods of time. This was also the case with patients who suffered from repetitive paranoid conflicts. Some of these patients managed to hold two jobs, which, in times of severe conflicts, enabled them to escape from one type of work to the other (see Jacobson, 1966b).

As long as these patients had a partner or friend around at home, they felt comparatively well and undisturbed, even if their relationships were as conflictual as those in the case I reported. But when these patients were faced with the prospect of having to spend an evening or a weekend alone, they would, as one of them said, completely go to pieces, unless they could fill up their time with work. I must stress the fact that the disturbances that these patients developed during such free periods basically did not resemble the "weekend neuroses" which we are used to seeing in certain neurotic, especially masochistic, patients. The psychotics to whom I refer were also unable to relax, rest, or enjoy any kind of sound, pleasurable activity. However, in contrast to neurotics, they would spend their free time in some kind of acting out.

Some developed the habit of going, immediately after their return from work, on drinking bouts and homosexual or heterosexual escapades. Those who stayed home felt so restless, panicky, and depressed that they drank steadily or ate throughout the evening. Some did not wash, shave, or dress on weekends and stayed in bed, sleeping, eating, drinking, and, at best, reading a thriller. During such periods some of these persons lost their sense of time or even developed feelings of confusion and unreality. A very impressive and characteristic feature was that, as in the case of Mr. A., these patients were generally regarded as competent, devoted workers, and sometimes even very charming, well-related persons. They managed to keep their alarming states well hidden under the screen of their seemingly well-adapted vocational behavior, which, in contrast to their repetitive impulsive acting out, showed rigidly compulsive features.

Many of these patients were aware of the fact that they clung so frantically and desperately to their work and the persons for whom they worked, and also to their lovers, friends, or partners, because these relationships kept them emotionally above water. In fact, a few of them promptly developed psychotic episodes when for external or internal reasons they were forced, or themselves decided, to give up a job or a personal relationship to which they had so stubbornly clung.

One divorced female patient in her late twenties remarried a very compulsive man who worked in the professional field in which she wanted to get a degree. Her close participation in his research and the strictness of his demands enabled her to finish her studies. But after some years she began increasingly to rebel against his compulsiveness and finally decided to leave him and also give up her work. "I cannot tolerate it any longer," she said. "He wants me punctually to pay our taxes, and he does not even allow me to entertain fantasies about getting at least six children." On the day of their separation she came to me for an interview, asking me to take care of her husband in the event that he had a breakdown because she had left him. This was a warning in the form of a projection. In fact, on the next day she went into a state of severe catatonic excitement and had to be hospitalized. Years later, after a long, comparatively healthy interval, the same patient formed a relationship with another professional man for whom she did secretarial work. Since he was married and refused to get a divorce, she again decided after some years to leave him and go to Europe, where she had another psychotic episode.

Another female patient had had recurring psychotic states from adolescence until the age of thirty. After recovery from the last episode, she managed, with the support of her psychotherapist, to find and to maintain a suitable job and, finally, to get married. She got along very well, except on weekends when her husband had to go on business trips and she did not have any regular scheduled activity. At such times she became anxious, restless, and depressed. In her middle forties, this woman decided to give up her job, which she had held without interruption for a period of more than twelve years. Some of the reasons were external, in part an increasing conflict with a superior who overloaded her with work. Her attempt to go into a different and easier field of work was not successful. She met with unexpected difficulties and failures, to which she promptly responded with a severe paranoid suicidal state of depression, once more requiring hospitalization.

In both these patients as well as in other psychotics whom I have observed, the choice of their personal objects and their professional activities played a significant role, as it did in the case of Mr. A. I wish to emphasize the point again that in spite of the inevitable conflicts with their partners and recurring problems in their work, these patients made remarkable efforts to adhere to the persons and the activities they had chosen, and succeeded in doing so for long periods of time.

However, the kind of reality that such patients need and the objects they select in their attempts to solve their conflicts vary greatly, depending upon the type of psychotic individual and the nature of the psychotic conflict. One such solution may be a turning to religion and active participation in the activities of a special church or sect.

One mildly schizophrenic, very anxious, self-conscious, depersonalized, shallow woman had constantly moved from one man, one job, one city, to another. Finally, in her thirties, she joined a religious sect which she had previously repudiated because her schizophrenic mother belonged to it. She became and remained a fervent follower and married a fellow sectarian, a widower with whom she has a close, rather symbiotic relationship in which the mystical belief they share plays a dominant role. She takes excellent care of his three very disturbed children and, in addition, works as a teacher. She lost her symptoms when she joined the sect and they have not recurred in her marriage. She has sustained her relationship with me, mainly by correspondence, for about twenty years, and last year she wrote me a touching letter, expressing her gratitude for letting her cling to me and for supporting her in joining this sect and marrying another follower. This had cured her, she said, because it had "taught her the meaning of love."

Another, very intellectual and very disturbed schizophrenic woman left her husband, and with her three children joined a commune, organized like those of the early Christians. There she was able to adjust, do missionary work, and teach.

A third patient, a young man of twenty, who at the age of five had already been diagnosed as a schizophrenic with a severe behavior disturbance, was baptized as a Mormon, his psychotherapist acting as his godfather. Since then he has been doing very well at the Mormon College in Salt Lake City.

Other psychotic patients use a political cause, scientific work, art, fiction writing, acting, and nature to prevent a psychotic breakdown and to maintain their psychic equilibrium.

One very sick homosexual patient, Mr. Z., whose case resembles that of Mr. A., was quite deteriorated and disorganized and drank heavily at the time he began treatment with me. Therapy did not make him heterosexual, but it enabled him to develop a good, enduring, though symbiotic relationship with a rather disturbed younger man, to stop drinking, and to take a scientific degree. He is now teaching and doing excellent research which has gained him a high reputation in his field. When he is separated from his friend, this patient has a tendency to go on homosexual escapades, which are regularly followed by states of panic and paranoid ideas of persecution. Mr. Z. is fully aware of the degree to which he needs his work, his students, and especially his friend, whom he regards as a "prerequisite" of his health. As was true in the case of Mr. A. and Charlie, Mr. Z.'s relationship to his friend is also very narcissistic. He, too, uses this young boyfriend and his students to externalize his conflicts and as a means of resolving them by primitive identifications. In his case, his creative functions and the highly abstract nature of his work play a very significant role.

I shall very briefly mention only two more examples: both men were heterosexual, married, borderline patients—one a writer, the other one a scientist. Both filled almost all their free time with work. When they had finished a piece of work and could not immediately find or start another challenging project, they developed states of severe panic. At such times they would indulge in extreme sexual acting out with women, in one case of a rather perverse nature. In neither case did these activities interfere with their work.

Neurosis and Psychosis

Instead of giving further examples I return to the question whether neurotic patients do not also try to resolve their conflicts by employing similar reality aids. I believe that more patients use this method of conflict solution than we generally realize, particularly acting-out patients and narcissistic types of neurotics.[6] I have earlier mentioned as an example the type of woman who tries to resolve her castration conflict by acquiring a man who un-

6 In an unpublished paper Dr. Seymour Post described the defensive function of acting out in neurotic patients.

consciously represents her penis. In other cases, a patient will attempt to externalize and resolve his superego conflicts by attaching his superego to his love object or to the analyst. These are the patients whose transference usually has a rather narcissistic quality and is characterized by introjective and projective mechanisms. However, a comparison of neurotics and psychotics shows the existence of conspicuous differences between them.

Even in very narcissistic neurotics, the superego, the ego, and its defense organization are far more solid than in psychotics. For this reason, the neurotic's acting out, in the transference and on the outside, does not have the same quality, even though it may also represent an attempt at conflict solution that involves external objects. Certain impulse-ridden hysterical patients have alternating periods of impulsive acting out and depression during which they "pay for their sins." On the whole, however, neurotics scarcely ever undergo such rapid shifts between compulsive and impulsive behavior, between comparatively good ego functioning in their work and wild acting out when they are alone—behavior so frequently observed in ambulatory psychotics.

The differences reflect the different nature and different functions of the external objects that by both neurotics and psychotics are employed for the purpose of defense. Neurotics as well as psychotics may have preoedipal-narcissistic fixations and suffer from severe pregenital and ambivalence conflicts. However, in the case of neurotics, the solidity of their psychic structures, the stability of their defenses—in particular of their *repressive barriers*— and the well-defined boundaries between self and object representations protect them from processes leading to drive defusion and drive deneutralization and to a flooding of the ego with sexual and especially with destructive and self-destructive forces to the point of a regressive dissolution of psychic structures. Because the neurotic's object relations are not on such a regressive narcissistic and sadomasochistic level, neurotics cannot even use the type of defensive operations I described in the case of Mr. A. and which I regard as characteristic of psychotics. When we encounter these defensive operations, we must suspect that we are dealing with a psychotic case.

To be sure, as I emphasized above, in my patient neurotic and psychotic traits, attitudes, and defenses were closely interwoven. He was also capable of maintaining rather normal personal relations with some people, but not with those who were involved in his acting out and used for the purpose of defense.

On the other hand, certain narcissistic neurotics also use primitive defenses, such as denial or introjective and projective mechanisms, which utilize external objects. However, they do not develop fusions between self and object images. Turning objects into parts of the self, or the reverse, precludes personal relationships on an advanced level. This is a very essential point which I shall take up again in the discussion of treatment problems.

Schizophrenic and Manic-depressive Psychosis

Although this lecture has been focused on schizophrenics, I want to discuss briefly how far the points I have tried to convey apply to manic depressives as well. My experience with a comparatively large number of patients who were in psychotherapeutic or psychoanalytic treatment with me because of periodic states of depression convinced me that what I have said about schizophrenics is, in principle, also valid for this group of psychotic disorders. Every one of these depressed patients attempted to employ the external world as an aid in the solution of his depressive conflicts and in the prevention of another depressive breakdown. However, the help from without that these patients need and want is of a different nature than in the case of schizophrenics.

First of all, the periods of remission in schizophrenics differ very much from the periods of remission in depressives. Despite the conspicuous mood vacillations, or the hypomanic conditions that some of these patients show between their depressive periods, their recovery is, in general, incomparably better than that of schizophrenics after a psychotic episode. As the case of Mr. A. exemplified, even during periods of remission, when schizophrenics function satisfactorily, or even excellently, their personality and conflicts remain basically psychotic in nature. The fragility and defectiveness of the superego and ego, the primitive narcissistic nature of the object relations that enables them to use the type of defensive operations I described, usually survive the acute episode to a greater or lesser extent.

In contrast, manic depressives, in their free intervals, re-establish not only normal ego functions, but also very warm, affectionate personal relationships. However, even though the ego and the emotional attitudes of manic depressives in periods of clinical health may not show the striking pathology that is generally observed in schizophrenics, other features remain very noticeable: their narcissistic vulnerability, their orality, their propensity for severe ambivalence conflicts, their superego pathology, and, hence, their need for narcissistic supply from without. These features, and especially the last one, are indicative of the kind of help which depressives want to get from the external world for the purpose of preventing another depressive breakdown. These needs become particularly conspicuous at the very beginning of a depressive period, i.e., before the withdrawal from the object world sets in.

In a paper on transference problems in the treatment of severe depressive cases (1954a), I called attention to the expectation of such patients that their love objects, and the world in general, offer them so much love and appreciation that they need not be ambivalent. This is the reason for their insatiable hunger for love. Two of my depressive patients expressed this in precisely the same way. They said: "Love, praise, and admiration are oxygen to me." In other words, melancholics want to employ their love objects for the solution of their severe ambivalence and guilt conflicts, which are caused by their hostility. In this same paper, I pointed to some of the implications that the analyst's attitudes have for such patients and to the difficult transference problems which result from their expectations.

Problems of Treatment

The "transference" reactions of schizophrenics can similarly be better understood if we realize how much and for what purpose they need and cling to the external object world. These considerations make us more aware of the complex, erratic, vacillating, and often contradictory nature of the relationship schizophrenics develop to their therapists (Searles, 1965a; Rosenfeld, 1965). In some patients, it may alternately be close and distant, dependent and autistic, touchingly clinging and frankly aggressive, cold and shallow and intensely demanding. These contradictory feeling qualities may be the reason for the existence of such different views about the psychotic's ability to relate and to develop a transference. The contradictory feelings are in part caused by the schizophrenics' current emotional state, the stage and the type of their psychosis; in part, they can be explained by the rapidly changing roles they ascribe to the persons to whom they attach themselves, and hence to the therapist.

This factor is of great significance for the treatment of schizophrenics, and particularly for the transference problems in those patients who are able to undergo a more or less modified psychoanalytic treatment.

At this point I must stress the fact that, although I have observed hospitalized schizophrenics in florid, acute, and chronic psychotic states and discussed treatment problems with their therapists, my own therapeutic experience has been limited to manic depressives and to ambulatory schizophrenics or patients during periods of remission from a psychotic episode. For this reason, my remarks on therapeutic problems refer mainly to the type of cases and the stage of illness during which they were in treatment with me. Unquestionably, the therapeutic methods must be adapted to the special type of psychosis—catatonic or paranoid, schizophrenic or hebephrenic. Apart from this consideration, however, the treatment problems during manifest delusional and hallucinatory psychotic states are certainly of quite a different nature than those encountered in cases such as the one I have presented. In spite of the variety of cases, it may be worthwhile to discuss briefly the general nature of transference phenomena in psychotics.

When we compare clinical case reports of such authors as Searles (1965a), Freeman et al. (1958, 1965), Rosenfeld (1965), all of whom have had a great deal of experience in the treatment of hospitalized severe psychotic cases, we notice, first of all, that the terms "transference" and in particular "psychotic transference" are used in rather different ways by these authors. Freeman, Cameron, and McGhie (1965) are remarkably cautious in employing this term. They carefully distinguish the "genuine, employable transferences [which are] similar to the transference neurosis of the neurotic reaction" (p. 58) from the "so called 'psychotic transferences' [which] result from an attachment of the predominant delusional complexes to the clinician" (p. 59). In their opinion, a patient who regresses to a "need-satisfying" level of mental functioning (A. Freud, 1952), "is incapable of transference, which is dependent upon neutralized object-libidinal cathexes" (p. 60).

These distinctions lose their meaning among analysts who are followers of M. Klein and who therefore believe that "the infant develops an object-relationship from birth onward both to external objects and through introjections to internal ones" (Rosenfeld, 1965, p. 106). If one adheres to the conviction that during the first months of life the infant passes through a period called "the paranoid-schizoid position," which is followed by the "depressive position," he must also assume that delusional psychotic symptoms will inevitably revolve around the therapist, and regard every psychotic reaction as an expression of true transference phenomena derived from the infantile past.

In Chapter 5 of *Psychotic States,* for example, Rosenfeld deals specifically with transference phenomena and transference analysis in an acute catatonic schizophrenic patient. He describes the first four sessions with a severely ill, delusional and hallucinating, dangerously impulsive, withdrawn, and at times almost mute patient, whom he treated for four months. I was particularly impressed by Rosenfeld's extremely skillful and intuitive understanding and handling of the patient in the first session. However, in the context of this paper, the other three sessions are more important, because they show that Rosenfeld begins almost immediately to give such patients what he calls transference interpretations, i.e., interpretations of their introjective and projective identifications with the therapist. From my previous remarks we understand that such interpretations—given routinely in this case and others he describes—supposedly refer to reactions which repeat the patient's relations to the mother during the first months of his life.

In the context of this lecture, it is not important that I do not share Melanie Klein's and Rosenfeld's opinions on this issue and that I am not even sure how far Rosenfeld's interpretations were always suitable. What is most pertinent to the context of this lecture, however, is that I used the same terms as Klein and Rosenfeld, i.e., the terms introjective and projective identifications, to characterize my patient's relations to those persons he needed as aids for his defense.

The question arises whether, in the case of my patient, these terms referred to the same wishes, impulses, and processes as those described, for instance, by Rosenfeld. This question points, first of all, to the differences in the mental life, and hence in the treatment, of manifest psychotic schizophrenic patients and latent psychotic patients, such as Mr. A. Moreover, there is the problem of the very different types of primitive identifications we can observe not only in different groups of psychoses but also at different stages of the illness. In an earlier paper on psychotic identifications (1954b), I focused on the distinction between the identifications of the melancholic, who treats himself as though he were the bad love object, and those of the delusional schizophrenic, who is convinced he has become another object. I also discussed the psychotic's regression to a narcissistic

level, where the weakness of the boundaries between self and object images gives rise to fantasies
or experiences of fusion between these images.
These primitive introjective or projective identifications are based on infantile fantasies of incor-
poration, devouring, invading (forcing oneself into), or being devoured by the object. We have no
means to explore the child's fantasy life during the
preverbal period; but we can assume that such
fantasies, which presuppose at least a beginning
distinction between self and object, are characteristic of early narcissistic stages of development and
that the child's relations to the mother normally
begin with introjective and projective processes.
However, such an assumption does not imply that
these processes are an expression of the infant's
defense against anxiety and of a paranoid-schizoid
or depressive position.

The differences in the types of what, in general
terms, we may call introjective and projective identifications depend upon the patient's fixation to
early narcissistic stages and upon the depth of
narcissistic regression and dedifferentiation of psychic structures. Although Mr. A. used primitive
projection mechanisms to turn Charlie into "his
penis, his id, a part of himself," he never showed
any sign of confusion between Charlie and himself.
However, I mentioned his fear that any affectionate physical contact might bring about experiences
of merging, which in turn might lead to a manifest

psychotic state. This is significant, because it points not only to the different, more or less regressive, kinds of primitive identifications which such patients establish, but also to the danger inherent in the defensive devices I described above. Although they depend on the choice of objects and the conflictual situation, these defenses may prevent the development of a manifest psychotic state; but such primitive identification relationships may also open the gate to further regression leading to fusions between self and object images, which might result in delusional ideas and a manifest psychotic state. This is what happened to Mr. A., both when he had a psychotic episode and for very brief periods during his treatment.

This leads me to some comments I should like to make on the treatment of ambulatory schizophrenic patients of this type, particularly those who are able to undergo a more or less modified psychoanalytic treatment. If we understand their defensive devices and the different roles in which they cast us, we can, at least during certain critical periods of our therapeutic work, lend ourselves to assuming these roles. I believe that some therapists who work with psychotics intuitively respond to their patients in this way. This explains the amazing transference successes that under these circumstances can be achieved with psychotics. Mr. A. was in treatment with me for about six years. Except for a period of preparation and certain critical phases, he had a genuine psychoanalytic experience which led to remarkable therapeutic results. During the initial period and, later on, during times of severe emotional crises, I permitted this patient to "use" me in the ways and roles that he needed. I adapted my emotional attitudes and behavior to his wishes, either for warmth and closeness or for more distance. I let him "borrow" my superego and ego; regard and treat me as his bad id and his illness; project his guilt, his faults, and weaknesses onto me; or turn me into the ideal of saintliness he needed.

During such periods, I avoided giving him deeper interpretations of his acting out in the transference or on the outside. I waited until he himself knew that the period of danger was over, and that he was ready to understand his reactions and behavior and the reasons for them. Only then would I also use the material he had previously brought for interpretations, which at such times would be surprisingly effective.

I know that my suggestions can easily be misunderstood in terms of my recommending the deliberate assumption of role playing (Alexander, 1950) and the employment of counterattitudes or even of involuntary countertransference reactions. For this reason, I want to clarify what I have in mind. In my discussion of transference problems in severely depressive patients (1954a), I mentioned that, in my experience, such patients did not work very well with therapists who tended to be detached rather than "warm" by temperament. The fact is that during healthy intervals manic depressives feel and show "warmth"; they want "closeness" and both need and respond favorably to warmth in the person to whom they relate. Their insatiable need for love is—at least in part—caused by their expectation that this love and appreciation will aid them in the solution of their intense ambivalence conflicts. It goes without saying that the analyst cannot and must not give them this kind of active "help." But this does not imply that the therapist must be devoid of that emotional warmth which enables such patients to establish a basically positive transference relationship.

In any case, a person either does or does not have "warmth" by nature. While it may depend on experiences of the past, it cannot be called countertransference, nor is it a counterattitude that can be deliberately assumed. The question is whether what I said about this problem in depressives is also valid in the case of schizophrenic patients. The answer is not so easy. In contrast to manic depressives, schizophrenics such as Mr. A., may at different stages of the transference situation, show a need either for more warmth and closeness or for the opposite, more distance. From the therapeutic point of view, I have found it extremely useful to adapt my emotional attitudes and behavior to the patient's wishes—that is to say, adapt them up to a certain point. However, what most schizophrenic patients need, besides, is a certain amount of strictness and discipline, which melancholics do not require. In fact, at least during certain stages of their illness and in periods of depression, schizophrenics, especially paranoid ones, may try their utmost to exploit other persons, including the therapist, with regard to time, money, practical support, drugs, etc. These attitudes have their origin in the patient's megalomanic ideas and his wish to adapt reality to his own wishes. If the therapist yields to such attempts on the part of patients to impose their wishes on the therapist, he will be lost. This is a special problem which I briefly discussed in a previous paper (1966b). In the context of this lecture it is important only insofar as it relates to my suggestion that the therapist lend himself to the roles the patient wants the therapist to assume. What I wish to stress is that this does not imply a suggestion to employ special counterattitudes beyond those I mentioned above. Nor would I recommend that therapist and patient develop an interrelationship of the sort which Searles (1965a), for instance, described in his papers on the treatment of schizophrenics.

Searles is certainly a brilliant observer and has probably the broadest experience, especially with severe hospitalized schizophrenic cases, where the treatment problems are in any event quite different in nature than in the group of ambulatory psychotic patients I have discussed. I share Searles's conviction that discussions of treatment problems with colleagues are of greatest value. However, although I admire the frankness with which he discusses his own countertransference manifestations, I must admit that I consider countertransference problems a private matter. Except in very general terms, their open discussion and public exhibition do not seem to me to be particularly useful. Such problems must be recognized and controlled in one's self-analysis or, if this does not work out, by re-analysis.

However, what I want to discuss are Searles's statements not about undesirable countertransference phenomena, but about those which he regards as valuable or even necessary for the treatment of schizophrenics.

In the chapter dealing with countertransference, Searles comments on the importance of the child accepting the incest taboo. These remarks are significant with regard to those reactions in the therapist which Searles considers therapeutically so useful. I agree with Searles's belief in the child's "ego-strengthening experience of finding that the beloved parent reciprocates his love." But I do not share his opinion that the parent normally responds to the child "as being, indeed, a conceivably desirable love-partner—and renounces him only with an accompanying sense of loss on the parent's own part" (p. 302). I should emphasize that Searles's remarks do not refer to the adolescent situation which, in ending the symbiotic relationship between parents and child, leads to reactions of grief on both sides. He speaks about the oedipus complex, about the child's renunciation of his incestuous wishes, and the corresponding renunciation on the part of the parent. That parents develop sexual desires toward their adolescent children is a frequent occurrence, but it surely is not a healthy phenomenon if parents develop such incestuous desires toward small children. I believe that as a result of such assumptions Searles tends to equate and to confuse symbiosis, mutual dependency, and love, including sexual impulses.

In Chapter 8, Searles states, for instance, that "what the therapist offers the patient . . . is not an *avoidance* of the development of symbiotic, reciprocal dependency upon the patient, but rather an *acceptance* of . . . the fact that the patient has come to mean a great deal to him personally. It is this acceptance of one's own dependency upon him that the mother had not been able to offer him" (p. 281). In Chapter 10, he says correctly that the schizophrenic patient must, in the transference, eventually regress to the symbiotic mode of relatedness. But he then states that this "is necessarily mutual, participated in by therapist as well as patient. Thus the therapist must come to experience not only the oceanic gratification, but also the anxiety involved in his sharing a symbiotic,

subjective oneness with the schizophrenic patient.
. . . Thus, at these anxiety-ridden moments in the
symbiotic phase, the therapist feels his own personality to be invaded by the patient's pathology,
and feels his identity severely threatened" (p. 339).

I have quoted Searles at some length because his
description of the interrelationship and interaction
between therapist and patient is precisely the opposite of my therapeutic suggestions. I believe that
if the therapist permits himself to establish a par-
ent-child relationship with the patient, which in-
cludes not only feelings of fondness and affection
but even parental incestuous desires; and if at a
certain stage of the treatment the therapist regresses along with the patient to a mutually symbiotic dependency—then the therapist will find
himself in dangerous situations which, in my opinion, are of no therapeutic value.[7]

To be sure, my opinion on this issue may not be

[7] In a critical review of my book on *The Self and the Object
World* (1964), Searles (1965b) expresses his suspicion that I am
afraid of symbiotic situations. I admit that I prefer oceanic
gratifications of a different nature to such experiences with patients. Although I have previously emphasized the extent to
which primitive identifications based on fusions between self
and object images normally survive and the part they play in
the empathetic understanding of other persons, I do not feel
that the analyst should permit them to develop to the point of
threatening his own feelings of identity. In fact, from my experiences in supervision and training analyses of students, I
must conclude that the propensity to establish symbiotic relationships that lead to identity conflicts presupposes an existing
tendency in that direction in the analyst.

valid with regard to severe hospitalized schizophrenic patients. Thus, I can only stress that in the group of ambulatory psychotic patients with whom I have worked, the type of mutual interrelationship and interactions which Searles describes appeared to be neither necessary nor desirable.

As a final point I wish to mention that in patients who rely heavily on reaction formations and have conspicuous compulsive traits and a basically intact ego, which make them accessible to a regular analytic process, the deep pregenital sadomasochistic id material comes to the surface only after years of treatment. One such patient, who had also had a psychotic episode, produced this kind of fantasy material readily and with the greatest ease in the very beginning of his treatment. When I interpreted these rather bizarre productions as a defense against his current conflict situation and his fears regarding the treatment, they stopped immediately. They reappeared years later, at which time they had genuine emotional meaning and could be interpreted and worked through effectively in the transference situation. In this case, as in the one I reported in detail, where severely traumatic infantile experiences had played a decisive role in the causation of the psychosis, the patients' personal emotional relationships as well as their attitudes to their work advanced to a much higher, more normal level, and their abilities to rest, to enjoy leisure, and to indulge in pleasurable activities greatly improved. So far, neither of these patients has had psychotic relapses. In both cases, the therapeutic results were much better than I had originally anticipated.

References

Abraham, K. (1924), A Short Study of the Development of the Libido, Viewed in the Light of Mental Disorders. In: *Selected Papers on Psycho-Analysis*. London: Hogarth Press, 1949, pp. 418-501.

Alexander, F. (1931), Schizophrenic Psychoses: Critical Considerations of the Psychoanalytic Treatment. *Archives of Neurology and Psychiatry*, 26:815-828.

——(1950), Analysis of the Therapeutic Factors in Psychoanalytic Treatment. *Psychoanalytic Quarterly*, 19:482-500.

Arieti, S. (1961a), Introductory Notes on the Psychoanalytic Therapy of Schizophrenics. In: *Psychotherapy of the Psychoses*, ed. A. Burton. New York: Basic Books, pp. 69-89.

——(1961b), The Loss of Reality. *Psychoanalytic Review*, 48:3-24.

Arlow, J. A. & Brenner, C. (1964), *Psychoanalytic Concepts and the Structural Theory*. New York: International Universities Press.

Bak, R. C. (1939), Regression of Ego-Orientation and Libido in Schizophrenia. *International Journal of Psycho-Analysis*, 20:64-71.

[65]

——(1949), The Psychopathology of Schizophrenia. *Bulletin of the American Psychoanalytic Association,* 5(3):45-46.

——(1954), The Schizophrenic Defence against Aggression. *International Journal of Psycho-Analysis,* 35:129-134.

Bellak, L. (1948), *Dementia Praecox.* New York: Grune & Stratton.

Bion, W. R. (1957), Differentiation of the Psychotic from the Non-psychotic Personalities. *International Journal of Psycho-Analysis,* 38:266-275.

Boyer, L. B. (1957), Uses of Delinquent Behavior by a Borderline Schizophrenic. *Archives of Criminal Psychodynamics,* 2:541-571.

Brody, E. B. & Redlich, F. C., eds. (1952), *Psychotherapy with Schizophrenics: A Symposium.* New York: International Universities Press.

Deutsch, H. (1942), Some Forms of Emotional Disturbance and Their Relationship to Schizophrenia. In: *Neuroses and Character Types.* New York: International Universities Press, 1965, pp. 262-281.

Eissler, K. R. (1943), Limitations to the Psychotherapy of Schizophrenics. *Psychiatry,* 6:381-391.

——(1951), Remarks on the Psycho-Analysis of Schizophrenia. *International Journal of Psycho-Analysis,* 32:139-156.

——(1953), Notes upon the Emotionality of a Schizophrenic Patient and Its Relation to Problems of Technique. *The Psychoanalytic Study of the Child,* 8:199-251. New York: International Universities Press.

——(1963), *Goethe: A Psychoanalytic Study*. Detroit: Wayne University Press.

Federn, P. (1952), *Ego Psychology and the Psychoses*. New York: Basic Books.

Fenichel, O. (1945), *The Psychoanalytic Theory of Neurosis*. New York: Norton.

Freeman, T., Cameron, J. L., & McGhie, A. (1958), *Chronic Schizophrenia*. New York: International Universities Press.

—— —— ——(1965), *Studies on Psychosis*. New York: International Universities Press.

Freud, A. (1952), The Mutual Influences in the Development of Ego and Id. *The Psychoanalytic Study of the Child*, 7:42-50. New York: International Universities Press.

Freud, S. (1911), Psycho-Analytic Notes on an Autobiographical Account of a Case of Paranoia (Dementia Paranoides). *Standard Edition*, 12:3-82. London: Hogarth Press, 1958.

——(1914), On Narcissism: An Introduction. *Standard Edition*, 14:67-102. London: Hogarth Press, 1957.

——(1915), The Unconscious. *Standard Edition*, 14:159-215. London: Hogarth Press, 1957.

——(1916-1917), Introductory Lectures on Psycho-Analysis. *Standard Edition*, 15 & 16. London: Hogarth Press, 1963.

——(1917), Mourning and Melancholia. *Standard Edition*, 14:237-260. London: Hogarth Press, 1957.

——(1922), Some Neurotic Mechanisms in Jealousy, Paranoia and Homosexuality. *Standard Edition*, 18:221-232. London: Hogarth Press, 1955.

——(1923), The Ego and the Id. *Standard Edition,* 19:3-66. London: Hogarth Press, 1961.

——(1924a [1923]), Neurosis and Psychosis. *Standard Edition,* 19:149-153. London: Hogarth Press, 1961.

——(1924b), The Loss of Reality in Neurosis and Psychosis. *Standard Edition,* 19:183-187. London: Hogarth Press, 1961.

——(1940), An Outline of Psycho-Analysis. *Standard Edition,* 23:141-207. London: Hogarth Press, 1964.

Fromm-Reichmann, F. (1939), Transference Problems in Schizophrenics. *Psychoanalytic Quarterly,* 8: 412-426.

——(1948), Notes on the Development of Treatment of Schizophrenics by Psychoanalytic Psychotherapy, *Psychiatry,* 11:263-273.

Frosch, J. (1966), A Note on Reality Constancy. In: *Psychoanalysis—A General Psychology: Essays in Honor of Heinz Hartmann,* ed. R. M. Loewenstein, L. M. Newman, M. Schur, & A. J. Solnit. New York: International Universities Press, pp. 349-375.

Greenacre, P. (1950), General Problems of Acting Out. In: *Trauma, Growth, and Personality.* New York: Norton, 1952, pp. 224-236.

——(1958), Early Physical Determinants in the Development of the Sense of Identity. *Journal of the American Psychoanalytic Association,* 4:612-627.

Hartmann, H. (1953), Contribution to the Metapsychology of Schizophrenia. In: *Essays on Ego Psychology: Selected Problems in Psychoanalytic Theory.* New York: International Universities Press, 1964, pp. 182-206.

REFERENCES

——(1956), Notes on the Reality Principle. In: *Essays on Ego Psychology: Selected Problems in Psychoanalytic Theory.* New York: International Universities Press, 1964, pp. 241-267.

Jacobson, E. (1954a), Transference Problems in the Psychoanalytic Treatment of Severely Depressive Patients. *Journal of the American Psychoanalytic Association,* 2:595-606.

——(1954b), Contribution to the Metapsychology of Psychotic Identifications. *Journal of the American Psychoanalytic Association,* 2:239-262.

——(1957), Denial and Repression. *Journal of the American Psychoanalytic Association,* 5:61-92.

——(1964), *The Self and the Object World.* New York: International Universities Press.

——(1966a), Problems in the Differentiation Between Schizophrenic and Melancholic States of Depression. In: *Psychoanalysis—A General Psychology: Essays in Honor of Heinz Hartmann,* ed. R. M. Loewenstein, L. M. Newman, M. Schur, & A. J. Solnit. New York: International Universities Press, pp. 499-518.

——(1966b), The Paranoid Betrayal Conflict. Read at Los Angeles Psychoanalytic Society and Institute.

Katan, M. (1950), Structural Aspects of a Case of Schizophrenia. *The Psychoanalytic Study of the Child,* 5:175-211. New York: International Universities Press.

——(1954), The Importance of the Non-psychotic Part of the Personality in Schizophrenia. *International Journal of Psycho-Analysis,* 35:119-128.

Khan, M. M. R. (1960), Clinical Aspects of the Schizoid

Personality: Affects and Technique. *International Journal of Psycho-Analysis*, 41:430-437.

Knight, R. P. (1939), Psychotherapy in Acute Paranoid Schizophrenia with Successful Outcome. *Bulletin of the Menninger Clinic*, 3:97-105.

——(1953), Borderline States. In: *Psychoanalytic Psychiatry and Psychology*, ed. R. P. Knight & C. R. Friedman. New York: International Universities Press, 1954, pp. 97-109.

Lidz, R. W. & Lidz, T. (1952), Therapeutic Considerations Arising from the Intense Symbiotic Needs of Schizophrenic Patients: In: *Psychotherapy with Schizophrenics*, ed. E. B. Brody & F. C. Redlich. New York: International Universities Press, pp. 168-178.

Little, M. (1958), On Delusional Transference (Transference Psychosis). *International Journal of Psycho-Analysis*, 29:134-138.

Mahler, M. S. (1952), On Child Psychosis and Schizophrenia: Autistic and Symbiotic Infantile Psychoses. *The Psychoanalytic Study of the Child*, 7:286-305. New York: International Universities Press.

Rosenfeld, H. A. (1965), *Psychotic States: A Psychoanalytic Approach*. New York: International Universities Press.

Searles, H. F. (1960), *The Nonhuman Environment*. New York: International Universities Press.

——(1965a), *Collected Papers on Schizophrenia and Related Subjects*. New York: International Universities Press.

——(1965b), Review of: *The Self and the Object*

World, by E. Jacobson. *International Journal of Psycho-Analysis,* 46:529-532.

Sullivan, H. S. (1953), *The Interpersonal Theory of Psychiatry.* New York: Norton.

Waelder, R. (1951), The Structure of Paranoid Ideas. *International Journal of Psycho-Analysis,* 32:167-177.

——(1960), *Basic Theory of Psychoanalysis.* New York: International Universities Press.

Wexler, M. (1953), Psychological Distance as a Factor in the Treatment of a Schizophrenic Patient. In: *Explorations in Psychoanalysis,* ed. R. M. Lindner. New York: Julian Press, pp. 157-172.

Winnicott, D. W. (1954), Metapsychological and Clinical Aspects of Regression within the Psycho-Analytical Set-Up. In: *Collected Papers.* New York: Basic Books, 1957, pp. 278-294.

Wisdom, J. O. (1963), Fairbairn's Contribution on Object-Relationship, Splitting, and Ego Structure. *British Journal of Medical Psychology,* 36:145-159.

Edith Jacobson, M.D.

Dr. Edith Jacobson was born in Haynau, Germany in 1897. After her graduation from the Realgymnasium at Liegnitz she attended Medical School at Jena, Heidelberg, and Munich. She received her medical degree from Munich in 1922. Dr. Jacobson served a pediatric internship at the University Hospital in Heidelberg and an internship and residency in Internal Medicine at the Munich University Hospital from 1922 to 1925. From 1925 to 1928 she served residencies at the Oppenheim Neurological Clinic and the Department of Psychiatry of the Charité Hospital in Berlin.

She received her psychoanalytic training during the same period (1925 to 1929) in the Berlin Psychoanalytic Institute. In 1929 Dr. Jacobson began a practice of psychiatry and psychoanalysis in Berlin where she became a member of the German Psychoanalytic Society. In 1934 she became a training analyst in the Berlin Psychoanalytic Institute. Not the least of the author's credentials was her imprisonment by the Nazis, shortly after Hitler came to power, for her refusal to give information about one of her patients to the Gestapo. Dr. Jacobson managed to escape from Germany in 1938. One of the happy derivatives of this nightmare episode were two papers on "Depersonalization" largely based on observations of fellow prisoners during her incarceration.

Dr. Jacobson came to the United States in 1938. In 1940 she began her private practice in New York where she became a member of the New York Psychoanalytic Society and Institute. She has been a training analyst of the New York Psychoanalytic Institute since 1942 as well as an active member of its faculty and Educational Committee. She is a past President of the New York Psychoanalytic Society and a Visiting Professor at the Albert Einstein College of Medicine in the Department of Psychiatry of Montefiore Hospital.

Dr. Jacobson is the author of numerous seminal contributions to the literature of psychoanalysis on a variety of clinical and theoretical subjects. Her recent book, *The Self and the Object World,* is a monographic synthesis of many of her original concepts of the structure of the "self," "self representation," and their relationship to "object representations" and object relationships. In *Psychotic Conflict and Reality* Dr. Jacobson brings years of practical experience and theoretical thinking to bear on a topic that she is pre-eminently qualified to discuss.

Publications by Dr. Jacobson

1927

Über die Einwirkung multipler Sklerose auf Narko-
lepsie. *Klin. Wschr.,* 6:1241-1242

1930

Beitrag zur asozialen Charakterbildung. *Int. Z. Psa.,*
16:210-235

Ein weibischer Knabe und seine Heilung: Charakter-
störungen und perverse Züge zufolge uneinheit-
licher Erziehung. *Z. psa. Päd.,* 4:291-298

1932

Entwicklung und System der psychoanalytischen For-
schung und Lehre. In: *Neue deutsche Klinik:
Handwörterbuch der praktischen Medizin,* ed. G.
& F. Klemperer. Berlin & Vienna: Urban &
Schwarzenburg, Vol. 9, pp. 274-318

Lernstörungen beim Schulkind durch masochistische
Mechanismen. *Int. Z. Psa.,* 18:242-251

1933

Review of: Aschner, B., *Klinik und Behandlung der
Menstruationsstörungen. Int. Z. Psa.,* 19:453-454

1936

Beitrag zur Entwicklung des weiblichen Kindwunsches. *Int. Z. Psa.*, 22:371-379

1937

Wege der weiblichen Über-Ich-Bildung. *Int. Z. Psa.*, 23:402-412

1943

Depression: The Oedipus Conflict in the Development of Depressive Mechanisms. *Psa. Quart.*, 12: 541-560

1946

A Case of Sterility. *Psa. Quart.*, 15:330-350

The Child's Laughter: Theoretical and Clinical Notes on the Function of the Comic. *The Psychoanalytic Study of the Child*, 2:39-60. New York: International Universities Press

The Effect of Disappointment on Ego and Superego Formation in Normal and Depressive Development. *Psa. Rev.*, 33:129-147; also in *The Yearbook of Psychoanalysis*, 3:109-126. New York: International Universities Press, 1947

1948

Review of: Sullivan, H. S., *Conceptions of Modern Psychiatry. Psa. Quart.*, 17:393-395

1949

Observations on the Psychological Effect of Imprisonment on Female Political Prisoners. In: *Search-*

lights on Delinquency, ed. K. R. Eissler. New York: International Universities Press, pp. 341-368

1950

Development of the Wish for a Child in Boys. *The Psychoanalytic Study of the Child,* 5:139-152. New York: International Universities Press

1952

The Speed Pace in Psychic Discharge Processes and Its Influence on the Pleasure-Unpleasure Qualities of Affects. *Bull. Amer. Psa. Assn.,* 8:235-236

1953

The Affects and Their Pleasure-Unpleasure Qualities in Relation to the Psychic Discharge Processes. In: *Drives, Affects, Behavior,* ed. R. M. Loewenstein. New York: International Universities Press, 1:38-66

Contribution to the Metapsychology of Cyclothymic Depression. In: *Affective Disorders,* ed. P. Greenacre. New York: International Universities Press, pp. 49-53

1954

Contribution to the Metapsychology of Psychotic Identifications. *J. Amer. Psa. Assn.,* 2:239-262

On Psychotic Identifications. *Int. J. Psa.,* 35:102-108 German: Über psychotische Identifikation. *Psyche,* 8:272-283, 1954

Transference Problems in the Psychoanalytic Treatment of Severely Depressive Patients. *J. Amer. Psa. Assn.*, 2:595-606

[Contribution to] Problems of Infantile Neurosis: A Discussion (Chairman, E. Kris). *The Psychoanalytic Study of the Child,* 9:49-50. New York: International Universities Press

The Self and the Object World: Vicissitudes of Their Infantile Cathexes and Their Influence on Ideational and Affective Development. *The Psychoanalytic Study of the Child,* 9:75-127. New York: International Universities Press

Federn's Contribution to Ego Psychology and Psychoses. *J. Amer. Psa. Assn.*, 2:519-525

1955

Sullivan's Interpersonal Theory of Psychiatry. *J. Amer. Psa. Assn.*, 3:149-156

1956

Interaction between Psychotic Partners: I. Manic-depressive Partners. In: *Neurotic Interaction in Marriage,* ed. V. W. Eisenstein. New York: Basic Books, pp. 125-134

1957

Denial and Repression. *J. Amer. Psa. Assn.*, 5:61-92

Normal and Pathological Moods: Their Nature and Function. *The Psychoanalytic Study of the Child,* 12:73-113. New York: International Universities Press

[78]

1959

Depersonalization. *J. Amer. Psa. Assn.,* 7:581-610

The "Exceptions": An Elaboration of Freud's Character Study. *The Psychoanalytic Study of the Child,* 14:135-154. New York: International Universities Press

1960

Review of: Cloward, R. A., et al., *Theoretical Studies in Social Organization of the Prison. Psa. Quart.,* 29:577-579

1961

Adolescent Moods and the Remodeling of Psychic Structures in Adolescence. *The Psychoanalytic Study of the Child,* 16:164-183. New York: International Universities Press

1964

The Self and the Object World [Journal of the American Psychoanalytic Association Monograph Series, No. 2]. New York: International Universities Press

1965

The Return of the Lost Parent. In: *Drives, Affects, Behavior,* ed. M. Schur. New York: International Universities Press, 2:193-211; also in *Canad. Psychiat. Assn. J.,* 11(Special Supplement):S259-S266, 1966

1966

Problems in the Differentiation between Schizophrenic and Melancholic States of Depression. In: *Psychoanalysis—A General Psychology: Essays in Honor of Heinz Hartmann,* ed. R. M. Loewenstein, L. M. Newman, M. Schur, & A. J. Solnit. New York: International Universities Press, pp. 499-518